The Life

あなたという生命、人生と愛、そして宇宙

Your Existence, Life & Love, and the Universe

Amy Okudaira

奥平亜美衣

光文社

The Life

あなたという生命、
人生と愛、
そして宇宙

Your Existence,
Life & Love,
and the Universe

目　次

✳

Contents

Chapter 1 ✳ Self

自分

あなたは、いつかなくなってしまう
有限の存在ではなく、
始まりも終わりもない、
永遠の存在、永遠の生命。

You are not a finite existence that will eventually disappear.
There are no beginnings or endings.
You are an eternal being and an everlasting life.

あなたは、
物質状態（生）と量子状態（死）を繰り返す
永遠の意識。

You are an eternal consciousness
that repeats your physical state (life) and quantum state (death).

本当は、あなたは、
生まれてもいないし、
死んでもいない。

The fact is you are not born or dead.

あなたは、ひとりの人間であると同時に、
無限の並行宇宙に遍^{あまね}く存在する無限の存在。
ひとり（粒）でありすべて（波）であるもの。
それがあなた。

You are a human being.
You are simultaneously an infinite being,
An individual being (a particle) and everything (waves)
prevailing in the infinite parallel universe.
That is you.

あなたは宇宙であり、宇宙はあなた。
この宇宙にあなたでないものは何もない。

You are the universe and the universe is you.
There is nothing else except you in this universe.

世界は、あなたの現れ。

あなたを映す鏡。

The world is a reflection of you.
It's mirroring you.

あなたの心は、「宇宙」の心。

あなたの意思は、「宇宙」の意思。

あなたは、自由意思そのもの。

Your heart is that of 'the universe'.
Your intention is that of 'the universe'.
You are free will itself.

宇宙は、あなたの中にある。
あなた自身が、あなたを内側から見ている。
人の数だけ、宇宙がある。

The universe is within you.
You are seeing yourself from within you.
There are as many universes as there are people.

あなたは人間という物質ではなく、
永遠に在り続ける空<ruby>空<rt>くう</rt></ruby>。

You are not a material object called a human being
but are eternal emptiness.

すべては空。
あなたも空。
あなたは、いつか空に還るのではなく、
今すでに、それそのもの。

Everything is emptiness.
You are also emptiness.
It isn't that you return to emptiness one day.
You already are emptiness itself.

わたしたちは永遠に、空であり、色。

We are eternally emptiness as well as form.

この宇宙を創造したのは、
あなたの「自分を知りたい」という意思。
宇宙を創造したのはあなた。
宇宙そのものがあなた。

This universe is created with the intention of you longing to learn about
yourself.
You created the universe.
The universe itself is you.

あなたも無限。

宇宙も無限。

無限の並行宇宙が存在して、

そこには無限の生命たちが輝いている。

そしてそこでは、

無限のあなたがあなたを知ろうとしている。

You are also infinity.
The universe is also infinity.
Infinite parallel universes exist.
Everlasting lives shine there.
And the infinite you is trying to learn about yourself there.

あなたは、
永遠なる存在がその永遠性を理解するために
地上に形を持って現れたもの。

You appeared here on this planet as a physical being
to understand the eternity of eternal existence.

あなたは、
始まりも終わりもなく在り続ける
自分を知りたいという思い。

You exist without beginnings or endings.
You are just longing to discover about yourself.

あなたは、愛であり、光。
そしてそれは神である。

You are love and light.
And it is God.

あなたを救えるのは、あなただけ。

Only you can save yourself.

あなたは、ただ、すべてを観ている。

You are just watching everything.

あなたは、どこまでも自由。
あなたを支配したり束縛したりする神はいない。

You are free in every respect.
There is no God who controls or restricts.

あなたは、静寂そのもの。

You are tranquility itself.

自分とは何か？

どうしてここにいるのか？

それこそが自分、つまり、神が知りたかったこと。

What am I?
Why am I here?
That is exactly what I, so-called God, wanted to know.

すべての人の人生は、
あなたのひとつの視点。
すべての人の人生は、
あなたの人生でもある。

Everyone's life is one of your perspectives.
Everyone's life is yours.

わたしから見たあなた
あなたから見たあなた
あの人から見たあなた
彼から見たあなた
彼女から見たあなた

The you seen from me.
The you seen from you.
The you seen from that person.
The you seen from him.
The you seen from her.

あなたは無限に存在すると同時に、
あなたという確固たるものは存在しない。
無限にいるけど、誰もいない。

You exist infinitely.
At the same time, you don't exist as a substantial being.
You exist infinitely but there is nobody.

なぜ生まれてきたの?

何のための人生なの?

その問いに対する究極の答えは、

なぜ自分が生まれてきたのかを知るため。

なぜ自分が生きているのかを知るため。

みんなそれを探して生きている。

Why were you born here?
What is this life for?
The ultimate answer to this question is
to eventually learn why you were born here,
and to know why you live. Everyone is living to chase the answer.

低次元から高次元まで、
すべての状態が自分の中にある。
あなたは多次元に多重に存在する。

From the lowest to the highest dimensions,
every state is within you.
You exist multi-dimensionally in multi-layers.

Chapter 2 ✳ Life

人生

人生とは、

本当は始まりも終わりもない

あなたという永遠の存在が、

生まれて死ぬという体験を自ら創り出したドラマ。

Life is like a TV series created by you
and lets you experience birth and death.
The truth is you are an eternal being
and there are no beginnings or endings.

あなたはドラマの役者であって、
その役は本当のあなたではない。

You are an actor in your TV series.
The character you are acting is not the real you.

あなたは、何者にもなる必要はなく、
ただ、あなたでいるだけでいい。

You don't need to be someone.
Just be you.

人生は、あなたが設定してきたゲーム。
その設定を思い出せば思い出すほど、
ゲームがスムーズに進む。
まるで攻略本を読んでいるかのように。

Life is a game programmed by you.
The more you remember the settings, the smoother the game will be.
Just like reviewing hint books about your life.

あなたの人生の設定を思い出すには、
「自分は何がしたいのか?」
それをただひたすら追求すること。

To recollect how your life is programmed,
just keep asking yourself 'what do I want to do?'
and simply continue with the quest.

人生はロールプレイングゲーム。

いきなり最終ステージには行けない。

目の前のミッションを確実にこなすことで、

着実にレベルが上がり、道が拓かれていく。

Life is a role-playing game.
You cannot go straight to the final stage all at once.
As you work on the missions in front of you,
you are steadily leveling up and new paths open up.

物事には流れや順番があって、
それを無視したり飛び越えようとしたりしても
上手くいかない。
ひとつずつ、
目の前のことをクリアしていくしかない。
クリアが必要なことはちゃんと目の前にやってくる。

Things move in order and with the flow.
It won't work out well if you ignore or skip over them.
All you have to do is to sort out things in front of you step by step.
What you need to resolve will definitely come to you.

人生にはシナリオがある。

そのシナリオは一本の線ではなく、

可能性の数だけ同時に重なり合って存在している。

その中でどれを選ぶか、

それは今あなたが出している波動で決まる。

Each life has a scenario.
The scenario isn't just one straight line.
There exist many available possibilities piling up at the same time.
The vibration you currently release will decide
which of the possibilities are chosen.

人生というのは、阿弥陀籤のようなもの。
阿弥陀籤の中にないルートは経験できないけど、
その中でどれを選ぶかは、自分の選択次第。

Life is like *Amidakuji,
You cannot experience a route that is not there, but
it all depends on you which option you choose.

*Amidakuji is a type of raffle popular in Japan when pairing with things or people.
It is structured with the number of vertical lines equal to the number of people playing and
horizontal lines which can be added by players. Each bottom end has a result. Each player
chooses a vertical line at the top and follows both the vertical and horizontal lines downwards
until reaching the bottom of the vertical line. It's named after Amida Buddha's Halo.

あなたの人生は、「変わる」訳じゃなくて、
そもそも決まっていない。
そして、あらゆる可能性が
すでに同時に存在している。

It is not that your life will 'change'
but it is not decided in the first place.
And there are various possibilities at the same time.

あなたは宇宙であると同時に、宇宙の1ピース。

そのピースの役割を果たす時、

すべてはピタリとおさまる。

自分がどのピースなのかを知り、それに沿って動く。

これが宇宙があなたに求めていること。

You are the universe and are simultaneously a piece of the universe.
When you fulfill the role of the piece.
Everything will fit right in.
Learn which piece you are and take the role of it.
This is what the universe is looking for in you.

人生のシナリオにあるものは、
必ず起こってくるし、
必要な人とは必ず出会う。

Whatever is in your life scenario will surely happen.
You will definitely meet people necessary for you.

人生には流れがある。

その流れに乗るだけで、

あなたは、あなたらしい人生を送ることができる。

There is a flow in your life.
You can live an authentic life just by going with the flow.

人生は常に、あなたを導いてくれている。

Your life will always guide you.

あなたにとって必要なことも、必要な人も、
全部必ずベストタイミングで
あなたの目の前にやってくる。
だから、何も心配いらないし、
安心して、人生を楽しめば大丈夫。

What and who you need will always come right to you
with the best timing.
So there is no need to worry. Feel safe and enjoy your life.

流れを信頼し、委ねましょう。

その流れそのものが本当の自分だから。

そうすれば、

ただこの人生を受け入れて楽しむことができる。

Trust the flow and leave yourself to it.
The flow itself is your authentic self.
That way, you can simply accept and enjoy this life.

自分本来の道でない方へ行こうとしたら、

ちゃんと、「出来事」が教えてくれるし、

止めてくれる。

その流れに逆らわないこと。

いつもあなたは守られているし、導かれている。

自分自身に。

If you move toward the path that's not for you,
there will be some 'event' to teach and stop you from going forward.
Don't go against the flow.
You are always protected and well-guided.
By yourself.

魂が求める道筋に必要なことは
必要な時に必ず起こって、
そして肉体はそれに逆らえない。

When a soul is pursuing a desirable path,
necessary events will certainly happen with the right timing,
and the physical body cannot go against them.

流れというのは、本当に正確に働く。
必要なことはちゃんと目の前にやってくるし、
必要無くなったら、瞬時に去っていく。

Flow works truthfully and accurately.
Necessary events come right in front of you.
If they are not needed anymore, they just leave instantaneously.

あなたが、本当のあなたは何者かを知れば、
人生に翻弄されるのではなく、
人生を楽しむことができる。

If you learn who you really are,
you can enjoy your life instead of getting tricked by it.

この人生で何をしたいの?
あなたはいつも、そう問われている。
あなた自身に。

What do you want to do in this life?
You are always asked that question.
By yourself.

疲れた時は、ひと休みすればいい。

人生はちゃんとあなたを待ってくれる。

Take a break if you feel tired.
Your life will wait for you without a doubt.

あなたがどうしようと、
喜びも悲しみも、
いいことも悪いことも、
生きることも死ぬことも、
あなたの人生にやってくる。

Whatever you do,
whether joy or sorrow,
good or bad things,
living or dying,
they all come into your life.

喜びも嬉しさも、

悲しみも怒りも嫌悪も、

すべて、必要だから起こっている。

Joy, pleasure, sorrow, anger, or hatred.
All of them happen because they are necessary.

Chapter 3 ✳ Happiness

幸せ

今ここで幸せを見つけることのできる能力が、
人間に与えられている最大の創造力であり幸運。

Our ability to find happiness here and now
is our biggest creative tool and the best luck given to humans.

幸せとは、あなたが感じるものであり、

誰かや状況がもたらしてくれるものではない。

幸せは常に、自分次第。

Happiness is what you feel.
It is not something others or situations would bring in.
Happiness is always depending on yourself.

どんな状況でも、その中にある幸せを見出すこと。
それが幸せを引き寄せる唯一の方法であり、
誰でも幸せを引き寄せることのできる方法。

In any situation, find happiness in it.
That is the only way to attract happiness.
That is the way for everyone to be able to attract happiness.

ただ、幸せであること。

それがあなたにできることであり、

唯一、しなければならないこと。

Just be happy.
That is what you can do.
That is the only thing you have to do.

みんなそれぞれ、生まれてきた目的が違う。

ゴールも違う。

だから、競争というのは無意味。

Everyone has a different purpose when they are born.
Each goal is not the same either.
Therefore, it is meaningless to compete.

それぞれがそれぞれの決めてきたことがあって、
それにただ向かっているとわかれば、
誰も、何も、羨ましくなくなる。

Each individual has their own decisions.
When they understand they are just moving towards them,
they will stop being jealous about anything.

社会的な成功が、魂的な成功とはまったく限らない。

成功は、自分自身の本当の喜びの中にある。

Social success is not always a soulful success by any means.
Success lies in the true joy of yourself.

今ここを天国だと思う人もいれば
地獄だと思う人もいる。
天国も地獄も、自分でつくっていて、自分の中にある。

One would think here and now is Heaven,
and another would think it is Hell.
Both Heaven and Hell are created by yourself,
and they are within yourself.

なんかいいことないかな、じゃなくて、

今日起こったことをいいことにする

Consider whatever happens today a good event,
and don't try to wonder 'is anything good happening?'

自分の幸せに自分で責任を取る。

これができるかできないかで、

人生は大きく変わる。

Take responsibility for your happiness.
Whether you can do this or not
changes your life dramatically.

幸せになれるか、というのは、

自分自身が幸せに気づけるか、見つけるか、感じるか、

だけにかかっている。

Whether you obtain happiness or not
depends on only whether you realize, discover or feel your own happiness.

宇宙にはすべてがある。

その中で何を見たいか、

それをあなたが選んで見ることができる。

Everything is in the universe.
You can choose and look at what you would like to see in it.

ないものを望むのではなく、あるものを喜ぶ。

これがあなたらしい人生を最高に幸せに生きる秘訣。

Don't wish for what you don't have.
Be pleased with what you have.
That is the key to living your own happiest life.

何にもしがみつくことなく、

ただ、あるものを喜び、

来るものを受け入れて、

去るものを追わない。

そうすれば、いつでも平穏が手に入る。

Without clinging to anything,
just appreciate what you have,
allow what comes in,
and don't chase what leaves you.
Then, tranquility always comes your way.

人生には、いいことも悪いことも起こる。
でもそのどちらも、
あなたに何かを教えてくれる。

There happen good and bad events in life.
Both of them will teach you something.

たとえ人生に問題が起きたとしても、
運命が順調に展開していると捉えることができる。
すべてはあなた次第。

If a problem arises in life,
you can take it as your destiny is unfolding smoothly.
Everything depends on you.

美味しいものを、美味しいなあ、ありがたいなあ、
と感じながら毎日食べているだけで、
運なんて簡単によくなっていく。

Your luck easily improves
simply by appreciating delicious food
and being grateful for daily yumminess.

人生を、いかに得るか、いかに成功するか、

いかに認められるか、いかに愛されるか、

から、

いかに楽しむか、いかに味わうか、

いかに自分を表現するか、いかに愛するか、

にシフトする。

You make a shift in your life
from
how you obtain, how you succeed,
how you get recognized, and how you will be loved,
to
how you enjoy, how you appreciate,
how you express yourself, and how you love.

あなたにとって、
あなた以外に、
何も特別なものはない。

There is nothing special to you except yourself.

すべては自分の中にある。

それに気づけば、

何も、恐れるものはなくなる。

Everything is within you.
If you become aware of it,
there is nothing to fear.

あなたには、

何も、恐れるものはない。

あなたが恐れなければ、

あなたは自由を手に入れられる。

There is nothing you are afraid of.
If you are not fearful, you are free.

幸せに正解はない。

There is no set solution to obtain your happiness.

願いを叶えても幸せになるとは限らないけど、
幸せになったら願いは叶う。

You don't necessarily become happy by making your wishes come true.
But if you become happy, then they come true.

Chapter 4 ✳ Desires

願い

この世は、
あなたがあなた自身の願いを叶えるために
あなたが創ったゲーム。
だからそれは必ず叶う設定になっている。
ただ、「あなた自身の本当の願い」を思い出すだけ。

This world is a game created by you
so as for you to make your desires a reality.
Therefore, they are programmed to come true for sure.
You only need to remember 'your true desires'.

あなたのやりたいことも、興味のあることも、
すでにあなたに内蔵されていて決まっているから、
ただそれに全面的に委ねたらいい。
ちゃんと、あなた自身があなたを導いてくれるから。

Everything is decided and built in you.
Say, what you want to do and what you are interested in.
You just entirely surrender to the setting.
Because you will guide yourself for sure.

本当にやりたいことなら必ず実現する。

誰かに見せるためとか、

優越感のためとか、

お金のためとかではなく、

本当にあなたのやりたいことであれば。

What you truly want to do will certainly become real,
if it is what you authentically want to do,
and if it isn't something to show others,
for your feeling of pride, or for money.

決めてきたシナリオ、
つまり自分が本当にやりたいことに沿って
自分が踏み出せば、
必要なことはすべて整えられていく。

The scenario is what you decided to be.
In other words, if you move forward based on what you truly want to do,
everything you need is arranged as you go.

自分と自分の人生に
設定されていないものを欲しがったら、
人生は苦しくなる。
自分と自分の人生に設定されているものを
<ruby>謳歌<rt>おうか</rt></ruby>したら、人生は最高になる。
人生に設定されているものは、
必ずあなたの前に現れる。

Your life gets painful if you desire what is not programmed in your life.
Your life becomes the best version
if you glorify what your life is set up for.
What is programmed in your life will manifest in front of you for sure.

もし、何か辛いことがあるとして、
それは、あなた自身が
いるべきところにいないから、
もしくは、あなた自身に設定されている
もの以外のことを願うから。

If something difficult happens to you,
it's because you are not where you are supposed to be.
Or, you are asking for something not programmed in you.

現実が嫌だ、不満だ、と思う人は、

まずは今ある幸せに気づき、

そこから抜け出すことが先。

現実が変わって望みが叶うのはその後。

必ず、内面の変化が先で、現実は後からついてくる。

現実は、絶対に先に変わってくれない。

If you don't like reality and have a bitter complaint about it,
you first have to get out of the scenario
by noticing your happiness at this moment.
Then after that, reality starts changing
and your desire comes true.
Your inner side always changes first and reality follows later.
Reality will never change first.

「自分は何をしたいのか?」
そこに意識を向け、
とことん考え、できることから行動する。
そうすれば自分が本当に望む人生が展開されていく。

Focus your consciousness on 'what do I want to do?'
Think it through and start with what you can do.
Then your life will open up in the direction you truly desire.

どんな小さなことでも、

今、やりたいと思うことを実行に移していく。

その積み重ねが、あなたを、

本来のあなたの道へと導いてくれる。

Any trivial things you think of,
just act based on what you want to do.
As your actions add up, you will be directed to your authentic self.

自分の中にある
「自分は何がしたいのか?」
「自分はどう生きていきたいのか?」
それを見つめ続けることが何よりも大事。

It's most important to keep asking yourself these questions:
'What do I want to do?'
'How do I want to live my life?'
The answers are within you.

どうなりたいか、ではなく、

何をしたいか?

そこに、あなたの願いがある。

It is not what do you want to become?
It is what do you want to do?
Your desire hides in the question.

人生は波乗り<ruby>サーフィン</ruby>。

波は何もしなくても勝手にやってくるけど、

そこに自分が乗らなくてはいけない。

あなたが波に乗りさえすれば、

自動的に本当に望んでいたところへ運ばれていく。

Life is like surfing.
Waves come on their own without your actions.
You will have to ride on them.
As long as you go on the waves,
you will be automatically sent to the direction you truly desire.

ないものを引き寄せるのではなく、
あなたの中にあるものを映していく。

It is not that you attract what you don't have.
You are projecting what you already have within you.

引き寄せとは、
願いが叶って幸せになる魔法ではなく、
叶っていなくても、
幸せを見つけたら幸せが返ってくる魔法。

The Law of attraction is not the magic to become happy
by making your wishes come true.
It means more happiness will return to you if you can find happiness
even before your wishes come true.

未来を設定して
その未来を引き寄せようとするのではなく、
ただ、今、幸せを選択する。
そうしたら、
自分の頭で考えたものをはるかに超えるような
幸せな未来を引き寄せる。

It isn't that you set up your future and try to attract it.
You only need to choose being happy now.
By doing so,
you will attract even more happiness far beyond your thoughts.

引き寄せとは、
都合よく思い通りに事を起こすことではなくて、
すでに思い通りだということを
理解して受け入れること。

The Law of attraction is not about how you make things
happen at your convenience.
It is about understanding and allowing that things have already
manifested as you like.

無理に「決めた」願いは叶わない。

叶うのは、それが叶うのを

「知っている」という感覚になるもの。

If you try to forcibly 'decide' on a desire, it will not come true.
When a desire is realized, it is like you have a sense of 'knowing' that
it was going to come true.

この世界には、どんな願いでも叶える方法はある。

だからこそ、

自分の本当の願いを知っていることが大事。

本当に望んでいないことを叶えても、

大変になるだけだから。

本当の願いを知れば、それを叶える方法は

自ずとその人の目の前に現れる。

There is always a way to make any of your desires come true
in this world.
That is why it is very important to know your real desires.
You will have only a hard time if you manifest what you don't want.
If you know your true desires,
you will automatically come across the ways to make them a reality.

こうしたら願いが叶うかな、叶わないかな、
なんて考えなくて大丈夫！
何をしたとしても、願いが叶うとしたら、
じゃああなたは何をする？

Will my desires come true or not if I do this?
There is no need to think about it!
What will you choose to do if they come true no matter what you do?

あなたが本当に望んでいることは叶うのだから、
本当にやりたいことをやりたいようにやれば大丈夫。

What you truely desire will come true.
So it is ok to choose what you want to do in the way you like.

あなたはいつも、自分の見たい世界を見ている。

You are always looking at what you want to see.

そして振り返ったら、
すべての願いは自然に叶っている。

When you look back, all of your wishes automatically came true.

本当にやりたいことなら
いつからでも何でもできる。
あなたの可能性は無限。

If it is what you really want to do,
You can start anything anytime.
You have infinite possibilities.

状況を改善しようとしたら、
望まない状況に意識が向く。
自分が何をしたいのかに意識を向けたら、
望む状況に意識が向く。
意識を向けたものをあなたは引き寄せ、経験する。

If you attempt to improve and control a situation,
your consciousness will be dragged to the undesirable.
If you go within and focus on what you want to do,
your consciousness will be drawn to the desired.
You will attract and experience what your consciousness is turning to.

何が起こるかというのはどうでもいいこと。

何が起こっても、あなたはその中から

自分の望むものを引き寄せることができる。

It doesn't matter what will happen.
Whatever happens,
you can attract what you desire from the event.

願いが叶った、と思ってもそこはゴールではなくて、
いつでも道の途中。
先のことはわからない。
先の願いより、その一日を精一杯楽しく生きること、
目の前のやるべきことをひとつずつやること。

When your desire comes true,
it means you are on the right path but are not at a goal yet.
You won't know about the future.
Live and enjoy fully for the day instead of thinking about future desires.
Work on what you need to do,
what is right before your eyes, step by step.

起こることに対し、その流れを信頼すれば、
人生に過不足がなくなる。
これが引き寄せの最終形。

If you trust the flow in every event happening to you,
you would feel enough and just right in your life.
This is the final form of the law of attraction.

あなたはすべて。

だから、本当はあなたは何も求めなくてもいい。

あなたに必要なものは、すべて与えられている。

You are everything.
So the truth is you don't have to ask for anything.
Everything you need is given.

あなたがあなた自身を発揮していけば
物事は自然に展開される。
誰にも邪魔されることのない、
あなただけの道。

If you unleash your own authentic self,
things unfold naturally.
It is your own unique path and it will not be disturbed by anyone.

自分を大きく見せることなく
かといって卑下することなく、
自分の本当にやりたいことに前向きに取り組む。
これがあなたがあなたの願いを叶える最短最善の道。

Without bragging or degrading yourself,
just positively work on what you truly want to do.
This is the quickest and best way to realize your desires.

現実を変えたければ、自分を変える。

それしかない。

そして、それができるかは、

自分＝宇宙という認識を持っているかどうか。

If you wish to change the current reality, change yourself first.
That's the only way.
And whether that can happen or not depends on
whether you have a perception of yourself = the universe.

Chapter 5 ✳ Reincarnation, Karma, and Fate

輪廻、カルマ、縁

この世は、あなたが見ている壮大な夢。

その夢の中で、

あなたは果てしない数の輪廻転生を繰り返してきた。

何のために？

それは、夢から覚めるため。

自分とは何かを知るため。

This world is a magnificent dream that you are watching.
In this dream, you repeatedly had endless cycles of reincarnations.
For what?
It is for you to be awakened from your dream state,
to learn what you are.

輪廻転生とは、ひとつのゲームを終え、
また別のゲームをやること。

Reincarnation means completion of one game
and moving on to a different one.

何度も何度も、
幾つもの異なった身体で人生を繰り返す。
それはただ、自分を知るため。
自分とはすべてなのだと知るため。

So many times,
you would repeat various lives in numerous different bodies.
This is solely for you to know who you are,
to learn you are everything.

この世界はあなたが創ったし、
あなた自身なのだけど、
それを忘れて、生死を繰り返すのが輪廻。
思い出したら、あなたは創造者に戻る。

The fact is you created this world and it is yourself.
But reincarnation lets you forget it and repeat life and death.
When you remember the fact, you will return to the Source.

自分自身に辿り着くまでの道は、
気の遠くなるほど長く険しいものである。

The pathway to reach yourself is so unbelievably long and strenuous.

しかし、自分を知りたい、という
意思さえ捨てなければ、
その道のりの途中で、
導いてくれる人や地図に必ず出会える。
そうしてあなたはいずれ、
果てしない転生の末に自分自身に辿り着く。

However, if you stay with an intention of longing to know about yourself,
you will definitely come across maps and people
that will guide you along the way.
And eventually,
you will arrive at yourself at the end of endless reincarnations.

あなたが自分の正体に辿り着いた時、
それが輪廻の終わりを迎える時。

When you reach your true nature,
that is the time to end your cycle of reincarnation.

死は存在しない。

死が訪れても、あなたは終わらない。

だから、死を恐れる必要はない。

Death doesn't exist.
Even when it comes, your existence doesn't end.
Therefore, you don't have to be afraid of death.

カルマとは、あなたが残した思い。

あなたが今生、成し遂げようとする思い。

Karma is the remnants of your thoughts.
They are the thoughts that you want to achieve in this life.

人生のシナリオを遂行するにあたって、
必要な人たちがいる。
それが縁がある人である。

To carry out your life scenario, necessary people exist.
You are linked to them by fate.

自分の人生のシナリオがあり、
それに必要な人とは
必要な時に自然と近づいていくし、
必要ない人とはどうやっても一緒にいられない。
無理にいようとすると、
色々と大変なことが起きる。

There is your own life scenario.
Necessary people will naturally come close at the right timing.
It is impossible to be with unnecessary people no matter what.
If you force yourself to be with them, you will be in a variety of trouble.

縁がある人とはあるし、ない人とはない。

そこは努力ではどうにもならない。

与えられた縁に感謝して楽しむのみ。

Some people are linked by fate and others aren't.
You cannot create such connections with effort.
Just appreciate and enjoy the given fate of connections

人間関係に固執しないこと。
あなたにとって本当に必要な人とは
ちゃんとつながるし、
残っていくから。

Don't hold on to human relationships.
You will get and stay connected to those who are truly necessary for you.

あなたに必要な仕事も縁も、

あなたにちゃんと回ってくる。

それが、人生の仕組み。

自分が引き寄せた縁を信じる。

Jobs and connections destined for you will certainly come your way.
This is the mechanism of life.
Just believe in the fate you attracted.

良縁も悪縁も、あなたにとって必要だからある縁。

Good and evil fates exist because they are necessary for you.

あなたが幸せでいられる人、
というのは、
あなたを幸せにしてくれる人ではなくて、
あなた自身がその人との関係性の中で
幸せを感じることができる人。

A person you can stay happy with is
one who you feel happiness with because of the relationship,
rather than expecting that person to make you happy.

信頼とは、

誰かが、自分を幸せにしてくれると

期待することではなく、

何が起きてもあなたがその人を信じること。

Trust means you believe in someone regardless of what happens,
and not expecting that person to make you happy.

あなたがあなたの道を歩むために、
あなたに必要な人とは自然と近づき、
必要無くなったら、自然と遠のく。

To walk on your own path,
you naturally become close to people necessary for you.
When they are not needed anymore, they naturally move away from you.

今出会っている人の中に、
あなたに今の時点で必要な人は、みんないる。
足りないものはない。

For this moment, all the necessary people already exist
among those you have met.
There is nothing missing.

ただ、自分をチューニングするだけ。
自分自身を高い次元にチューニングすれば、
本来の自分に必要なものにつながり、
必要のないものを遠ざける。

All you have to do is to tune yourself.
If you tune yourself into higher dimensions,
you will be connected to those necessary for your authentic self
and deter what you don't need.

見えている現実は、すべて過去。
それがわかれば、
現実を変えよう、他人を変えようという
無駄な努力はしなくなるはず。
過去は、変えられない。

Every reality you see is all in the past.
If you become aware of it, let's change your reality.
You will stop useless efforts, say, changing others.
You cannot change your past.

人を変えようとしても絶対に変わらない。

あなたの「変えなければいけない人」という思考が

現実を創るから。

人を変えたい、と思わなくなった時、その人は変わる。

人を変えたければ、

自分の考え方を変える以外にない。

You can never change other people even if you try to.
Because your thought, 'a person that needs to be changed'
will create a reality.
When you stop thinking about changing a person,
the person will change.
If you want to change others, the only way is to change how you think.

自分が罪悪感を抱くようなことはしない。
それがあなた、そして、
全並行世界に無数に同時に存在するあなたに、
望まないものが返ってこないようにする方法。

Don't do what you feel guilty about.
This is the way you,
who also exist simultaneously in numerous parallel realities,
can avoid receiving what you don't want.

世の中に、悪い気や念はある。

しかし、自分の心が

それを受け取らないような状態だったら、

それを引き寄せることはない。

There are bad energies and thoughts in the world.
However, if your heart is in the state of not catching them,
you will not attract them.

Chapter 6 Love

愛

あなたの本質は、愛であり、光。

Your true nature is love and light.

愛とは、本当の自分の姿。

Love is the actual appearance of you.

愛とは、すべてであり、
光と闇の両方を内包するもの。

Love is all that is.
It involves both light and darkness.

光も、闇も、善も悪も、
すべてはあなたの中にある。
そのうちどれを表現するかは、あなたの自由。

Light, darkness, good or evil, all are in you.
It's up to you which elements to express.

光とは、

自分自身の中にすべてがあると気づくこと。

闇とは、

自分の不幸を環境や人のせいにしていること。

Light means becoming aware of having everything within you.
Darkness means blaming the environment and
other people for your bad fortune.

あなたを裁く神は存在しない。
神とはすべてであり、愛であり、
それはあなたのこと。

There is no God that judges you.
God is all and love.
It means you.

神とか仏というのは
どこかにいる尊い偉い存在ではなく、
最高次元のあなたのこと。
そして、それが愛である。

God or Buddha are not venerable or high-up existing somewhere else,
but they are you at the highest dimension.
And it is love.

あなたが本当に救われるのは、
あなた自身を思い出した時。
それ以外にはない。
だから、自分自身についての真実を伝え、
思い出させること。
それこそが、愛である。

When you are truly saved, it is when you remember who you are.
There is no other solution.
Therefore, tell the truth about yourself and allow yourself to recall it.
That is exactly love.

Chapter 7 ✳ Awakening

目覚め

世界は、あなたがあなたを思い出すために、
あなたが創造した、壮大な仮想現実。

The world is a magnificent virtual reality,
created by you for you to remember who you are.

この世界は、あなたの中。
あなた自身が反映させた夢であり、幻。

This world is within you.
It is your reflection of dreams, and also an illusion.

何もない空である自分が、無数の分身を創り、
仮想現実世界で肉体を纏って
人生ゲームをしているのが今。
何のゲームかというと、
自分＝宇宙（すべて）＝愛ということを
知るためのゲーム。

You, emptiness with nothing, create numerous alter egos.
Right now you are playing your life game
with a physical body in virtual reality.
What is the game about?
A game to learn about Self = The universe (whole) = Love.

この世は幻想であり、ドラマであり、ゲーム。

それを見抜くのが解脱。

しかし、解脱してもゲームからは降りられない。

幻想だとわかった上でどう生きていくか。

それはあなた次第。

This world is an illusion, like a TV series or a game.
Recognizing it means 'gedatsu', or eternal liberation.
However, you cannot quit the game even after then.
How will you live after discovering the illusion?
It depends on you.

自分とは何かを知るために、世界が必要だった。
だから、世界が生まれた。

To know what I am, I needed the world.
Therefore, the world was born.

自分とは何かを知るために、肉体が必要だった。
だから、肉体が生まれた。

To know what I am, I needed a physical body.
Therefore, the physical body was born.

自分とは何かを知るために、
言葉や文字が必要だった。
だから、言葉や文字が生まれた。

To know what I am, I needed words and phrases.
Therefore, words and phrases were born.

自分とは何かを知るために、
それを教えてくれる人や書物が必要だった。
だから、時間が生まれた。

To know what I am, I needed the people and books to teach me.
Therefore, time was born.

　自分が自分を知りたいと思った時、
すべてが生まれた。

Everything was born when I thought I wanted to know about myself.

目覚めとは、
あなた自身も、あなたのいるこの世界も、
仮想のものであり、
その本質は目に見えない
「情報」なのだということに気づくこと。

Awakening means you and this world are in a virtual reality,
and also means becoming aware of its core nature being invisible
'information'.

宇宙はひとつじゃない。

あなたもひとりじゃない。

The universe is not only one.
You are not only one either.

自分の中に宇宙があって、
その中のひとりの人間の視点に入り込んで、
内側から宇宙を見ている。

There is a universe in yourself and
you are in the perspective of one human in it,
and watching the universe from within.

空<ruby>くう</ruby>であるあなたが仮想現実を創り出し、
その中で、
自分は空<ruby>くう</ruby>だと認識し続けるということが
延々と繰り返されているのが、
この宇宙の本当の姿。

You, emptiness, created a virtual reality.
In this reality, it is repeated endlessly for you
to continue recognizing you are emptiness.
It is the real appearance of this universe.

あなたは、自分とは何かを思い出すために、
すべてを忘れた。

You forget everything,
so as for you to remember who you are.

この世界は、
自分とは何かという問いであり、答えである。

This world is a question and answer of what I am.

あなたが本当の意味で満たされる時。

それは、あなたがあなた自身について知った時。

When you feel fulfilled for real.
It is when you know about yourself.

本当は、何も起きていない。

何も始まっていないし、終わってもいない。

時間も空間もない。

The truth is nothing is happening,
Nothing is beginning, nothing is ending,
and there is no time or space.

あなたがどこまで行ったとしても、
何をしたとしても、
あなたはあなたの中にいる。

Wherever you go,
whatever you do,
you are within you.

形のある世界で肉体を持ちながら、
形のない自分を思い出すこと、
それが目覚め。

Having a body in a physical world,
and remembering about non-physical self.
That is a state of awakening.

ゼロ（空）には、何もないけど、
すべての可能性がある。
そしてあなたも、空の可能性のうちのひとつ。

Zero (emptiness) is nothingness but has all the possibilities.
And you are one of the emptiness possibilities.

あなたは、世界そのもの、宇宙そのもの。

だから、失うものもなければ、得るものもない。

ただ、波が起こっては消えるだけ。

You are the world itself and the universe itself.
Therefore, there is nothing for you to lose or gain.
Just waves occur and disappear.

わたしたちは空（全体）であると同時に個。
あなたはいつか空に還るのではなく、
今すでにそうである。
そして、永遠に全体であると同時に、
永遠に個。それがあなた。

We are emptiness (whole) and individual at the same time.
It doesn't mean you eventually return to emptiness.
You are already emptiness.
And you are an eternal whole
and simultaneously an everlasting individual.
That is you.

あなたは、自由意思そのもの。
だって、自分しかいないのだから。

You are free will.
Because there is only you.

あなたのことを決めているのは、全部、あなた。
あなた以外の何かが決めているということはない。
あなたと分離した何かなんてないのだから。

Decision-making about you is all done by you.
There is no other way of making decisions apart from you.
Because there is nothing separate from you.

あなたはなぜ眠っているのか?

それは、目覚めるため。

Why are you sleeping?
So that you can be awakened.

あなたは、あなた自身を知るために、
今ここで、これを読んでいる。

You are reading this here and now
so as for you to learn about yourself.

世界には、目に見えるものは
本当に何も存在していない。
それが本当にわかれば、
静寂と平和と幸福が訪れる。

Visual things don't exist for real in the world.
If you understand this for real,
tranquility, peace, and happiness come along

人生は仮想世界に展開するドラマ。
そのドラマに飲み込まれるのか、
そのドラマを鑑賞して楽しむのか、
あなたが選択できる。

Life is like a TV series.
Whether you are drunk by it
or enjoy watching it,
you can choose.

すべての苦しみは、

自分が肉体を持つ有限のひとりの人間だと思い、

この世をリアルだと思うから起こる。

でも本当は、この世界はひとつのゲームであり、

あなたは無限。

All pain arises if you think you are a limited human
with a physical body, and this life is real.
But the reality is this world is a game and you are infinite.

この世の苦しみから逃れる方法はふたつ。

ひとつは、何が起こってもその中に、

喜びや幸せを見出すこと。

もうひとつは、この世界は、自分も含め、

実体がない仮想現実であるということに気づくこと。

There are two ways to deter pain in this world.
One is to figure out joy and happiness
within any situation that happens to you.
The other is to become aware of this world, including yourself,
as an insubstantial virtual reality.

この世界は、幻。

だから、この世界に囚われることは何もない。

ただ、あなたの生きたいように生きればいいだけ。

This world is an illusion.
Therefore, there is nothing to be swayed by.
All you do is live as you like.

あなたの中に、わたしがいる。

わたしの中に、あなたがいる。

あなたの言葉は、わたしの言葉。

わたしの言葉は、あなたの言葉。

I am within you.
You are within me.
Your words are mine.
My words are yours.

わたしの中にすべての人がいる。
わたしとあなたはひとつ。

Everyone is within me.
You and I are one.

Chapter 8 ✳ From now on

これから

誰が一番早く走れるかより、

走りたい人が楽しく走る時代へ。

We are in the time period for whoever wants to run for fun
rather than who will run and win the first prize.

これから来る世界は、量子技術によって、
物質やお金に対する価値観が
これまでと全く違うものになる世界。

Quantum technology will take off in the coming world,
and then the standard of values for physical matters and money
will be totally different.

目覚めた人だけが新しい世界に行けるのではなく、
それぞれがそれぞれの望む世界へ。

Each person will move on to a different world they desire,
rather than only awakened people can go to a new world.

一部の人が豊かさを蓄積した時代から、

みんなが豊かさをシェアする時代へ。

A new period will take off where everyone shares abundance
shifting from the time when only part of the population had wealth.

社会の変化が
あなたの現実を変えてくれるのではなく、
現実を選択する力を持っているのは常にあなた。
あなたの生き方がすべてを決める。

The social change will not change your reality.
It is always you who have the power to choose different realities.
The way you live will decide everything.

『IMAGINE』で歌われた世界は本当に来る。

そのためには、一人ひとりが

平和とシェアの心を持つこと。

The world sung in 'IMAGINE' will really come.
To create such a world,
everyone needs to possess a heart of peace and sharing.

目覚めたらすべてがよくなる。
光が勝てばすべてがよくなる。
これらは現実逃避なので、
ずっと逃避したくなるような現実を
引き寄せ続ける。

Everything becomes better if you are awakened.
Everything becomes better if light wins.
These are forms of escapism.
And they will keep attracting a reality of wanting to continue to escape.

宇宙人は地球を変えてくれない。
世界を変えるのは、あなたの心。

Aliens will not change the Earth.
Your heart will change the world.

世界がどうあったとしても、
自分は自分の道を行くだけ。
影響はあったとしても、
そこから何を選び出すかは、全部自分次第。
だから、世界で何が起こるかは、
自分の幸せや人生には関係がない。

Whatever is happening in the world,
you only have to focus on your path.
Even if something is influencing you,
what you choose from it all depends on you.
That is why what happens in the world
doesn't affect your life or happiness.

あなたは変化し続ける
永遠の存在。
これまでも、これからも。

You are an eternal existence that keeps changing
up until now and for eons to come.

理想郷は、手の届かないところにあるのではなく、

今、ここに重なって存在している。

The Utopia is not in an unreachable place, but
it exists and overlaps here and now.

救世主を求めても、

誰かが救ってくれるということはない。

あなた自身が、自分自身を知ろうという思い、

それこそが救世主である。

救世主は、最初から最後まであなたの中にいる。

Even if you ask for a savior,
it doesn't necessarily mean someone is going to save you.
it is a savior itself
when you have a thought of wanting to learn about yourself.
A savior is within you from the beginning to the end.

誰かが人々を支配しようとしても、
それぞれの心は支配できない。
心は自由。
自由な心で人生を楽しむこと。

If someone tries to control people,
the person cannot control their heart.
Your heart is free.
Enjoy your life with a free heart.

今すべてをわかろうとしないこと。

うまくいかないことがあっても、

いつか、あれでよかったとわかる日が来るから。

Don't try to understand everything now.
Even if things don't work out well,
one day you will know that was the best scenario.

自分とは宇宙であることを知ること。

すべては完璧であることを知ること。

自分の幸せを自分で選択すること。

自分の道を歩くこと。

それが、これからの生き方。

Learn that you are the universe.
Know that everything is perfect.
Choose your happiness by yourself.
Walk your own path.
That is the way to live from now on.

英訳
前田真弓

＊

ブックデザイン
鈴木成一デザイン室

＊

写真
Adobe Stock

奥平亜美衣

Amy Okudaira

✴

1977年兵庫県生まれ。お茶の水女子大学卒。
幼少の頃より、自分の考えていることと現実には関係があると感じていたが、
2012年に『サラとソロモン』『引き寄せの法則　エイブラハムとの対話』との
出会いにより、「引き寄せの法則」を知り、自分と世界との関係を思い出す。
当時、ごく普通の会社員だったが、
「引き寄せの法則」を知ることにより現実が激変し、
2014年に初の著書『「引き寄せ」の教科書』を刊行、ベストセラーとなる。
その後も著書は次々とベストセラーになり、累計部数は90万部を突破。
2020年4月、コロナ禍で自宅に引きこもっている間に、
「宇宙すべてが自分なのだ」という目覚めがあり、
無であり無限である「わたし」を思い出す。

The Life
あなたという生命、人生と愛、そして宇宙

2022年11月30日　初版第1刷発行

著者
奥平 亜美衣

発行者
三宅貴久

発行所
株式会社 光文社
〒112-8011　東京都文京区音羽1-16-6
〈編集部〉03-5395-8172〈書籍販売部〉03-5395-8116
〈業務部〉03-5395-8125
メール non@kobunsha.com

落丁本・乱丁本は業務部へご連絡くださMinValue, お取り替えいたします。

組版・印刷所
萩原印刷
製本所
ナショナル製本